The Changing Tides

Printed in New York by:

OMNIBOOK CO.
99 Wall Street, Suite 118
New York, NY 10005
USA
+1 202-738-1322
www.omnibookcompany.com

First Edition

For e-book purchase: Kindle on Amazon, Barnes and Noble
Book purchase: Amazon.com, Barnes & Noble,
and www.omnibookcompany.com
Omnibook titles may be purchased in bulk for educational, business,
fund-raising, or sales promotional use. For more information
please e-mail **info@omnibookcompany.com**

Cover Design by: Gian Carlo Tan

The Changing Tides

I'm just saying

JOHN **BOULEY**

Contents

The Changing Tides

We are all born into a world for which we never fully understand. Like the ocean, there are so many mysteries left to explore but there is never enough time. We live in the moment of our changing ways that makes it hard to grasp what or who we truly are. We become living metaphors of ourselves with the consistent obsolescence of everything we know, for what we have and what we truly understand changes so radically that somehow, we miss out on the true meaning of our lives. Is there a purpose of all this? What sense does it make if we leave this world not knowing who we really are or why we exist? Some believe in a deity that gives us a purpose after we're gone. Some believe through an evolutionary process we become who we are. But can our very existence somehow have fallen into the hands of chance? For there has to be more to it all and like the changing tides, we continue to exist without ever really knowing. For there is so much to learn and one of the great ways of obtaining knowledge is from each other through the literary progression of our minds pushing forward like the rushing tides changing at a rapid pace to hopefully, one day, fulfil the voids of an ever-changing world. I give you my poetry.

Just A Woman

I place in my mind the fundamentals of its nurture. I'm
intrigued by my sensitivity as if the epigram of my presentation
holds a purpose. I expose myself as if naked for the world
to scrutinize and motivate me, but I digress. I think about a
woman, candidate in her valor, provocative by nature, never
compromise by promiscuity or looked upon as impudent. The
true essence of femininity that takes me beyond my ability to
control my emotions, as if a child enchanted by the aroma of
a candy store. I think about her beauty, held captive by her
demeanor that paralyzes my ability to defer, frozen in the
moment of undying contentment, again, I digress. I think about
a woman waking up in the morning as if she were a flower just
planted in the early spring. As she rises to a new day in all her
splendor, she progressively becomes more vivid in my mind as
if the flower became in full bloom exuberating an aesthetic
botanical visual that touches my soul. I become the bee that
is incapable of its natural instinct to pollinate throughout the
fields of God's unwavering grace held only to her and drawn to
her by a power beyond my capacity to control. I look at myself,
a man created for the sole purpose of her pleasure, and by the
virtue of God's undeserving kindness given unto me I witness
the miraculous beauty that stands before me.
How then could I ever say she's just a woman.

The Thunder in the Distance

I can see ahead of me the ominous skies. The overwhelming feeling of some sort of Doom that impedes my optimism. I am humbled by its ferocity that drives my soul into an interlude of fears. Like the prophecies revealed in a revelation that promises the inevitable plight. I am caught up in its evidences, a world wrapped around its stigma as its chaos is inoculated into the ignorant, the vulnerable, soon condemnation as if it were telling the blind to go into a light of which they will never see. The falsehoods of the overly convincing that tends to dominate in a system that needs to end. As I hear the loud thunder clap over my very existence though temporary, I can't help but think so precious is my life as if it is being threatened by this natural phenomenon. As unspeakable voltage illuminates a vast horizon, I'm caught up in its worst praying for a resolution that will probably never come as a drenching monsoon surrounds me with intolerance. I try to imagine the world after the storm as a promise starts to break through giving hope of peace and comfort but I am disillusioned by its temporary status. As I lay here in the Maelstrom of it all, the storm passes. I feel a false sense of tranquility, still knowing that soon it will return, for in a world that exist with so much hatred, there's always a threat of a storm and if you listen closely with humility in your heart, you will hear the thunder in the distance.

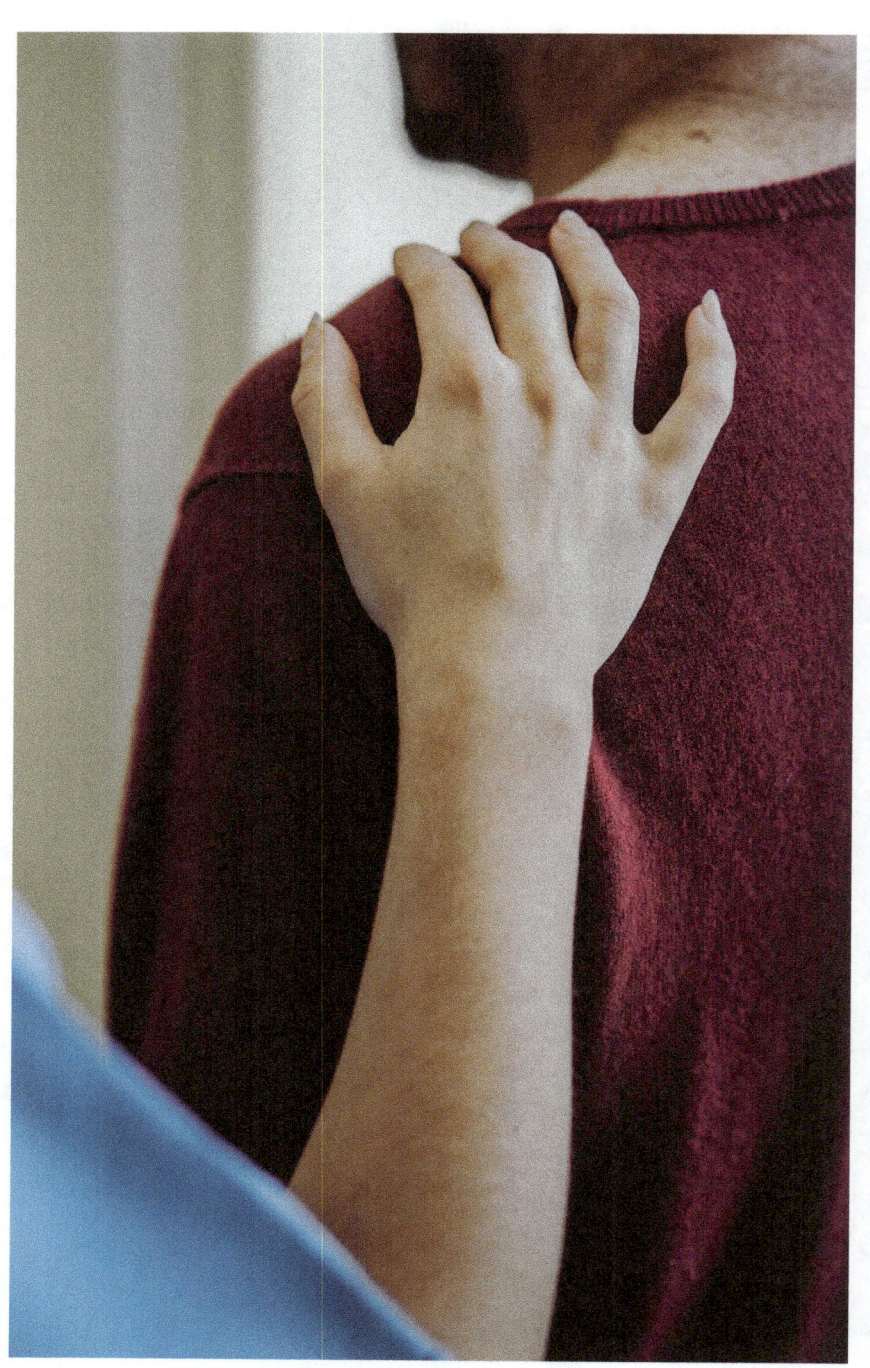

The Impervious Battle

In all wars, the soldier prays for a resolution of peace, for who is it that has more to lose. We all have a battle to fight that's not always on the battlefield, for never giving up gives you strength to deal with whatever comes your way, for then we become soldiers so begins the impervious battle. I will not let this disorder consume me for I will become the impenetrable. My resources are prayer and faith, for who is it that goes to war unarmed. Lord I ask for the right words to pray so that you can help me cope with this infirmity. For I will stand up right in the face of the battle with all my might and heart. I believe the road to fulfillment begins with reverence for my deity and whatever is decided upon me, for blessings will be bestowed upon those with faith. I will advance confidently with the hopes and prayers that will give me the strength that I need and by the endearment of others that surround me. I will walk the Battlegrounds with confidence for this insurrection of disorder is only a temporary status. For no war has ever been won by its first battle but by belief that there is something greater than ourselves, we can gain strength beyond ourselves to continue to fight this anomaly that will not take me down making this my impervious battle.

The Weight of the World

If I was to step out of my soul right now and look at myself,
I wouldn't recognize me.
Sometimes I feel so helpless,
so vulnerable in the hands of the world.
Where did all this rain come from
looking for the sun that all I see is clouds.
My feet are so tired of running away from what is implied for,
is it you I owe this obligation?
Whereas, to whom do I need to ask
 to search and find myself again if not me.
It gets so cold outside sometimes
looking for the comfort of yet another day hurting,
being told it's not that bad.
When did you take lease inside of me?
Absence of you I take hold but yet not without exit of pain,
or do I continue in the rain.
If I say I'm sorry will you understand, for not likely.
Do you see me holding up the weight of the world?
Or did you not see it on my shoulders.
I never meant to hurt you.

The Exotic Dancer

Once brought up to be inhibited the change from childhood innocence, transforms itself. As the paradox plays out in her commitment to chastity that eventually becomes dubious by a divergence that implores the soul's natural instinct to become somewhat carnal. By the reflection of her physical form, she becomes vivacious with an immense willingness to share. She is described as this, thin but curvaceous with a bosom that symmetrically compliments her supple aesthetics. The apogee of beauty in-motion as her body rhythmically sway's audaciously to a steady interlude of repetitious percussion. The audience is set with dauntless anticipation as a feminine silhouette of such stunning physicality appears through a small threshold covered with silk curtains. Her heart beating profusely knowing that her exposure, though profound, opens up a whole new world for this is her first dance in front of aroused spectators. Such an overwhelming feeling of consternation, as these ambivalent thoughts pervade, she simultaneously moves through the portal, like jumping into an ice-cold ocean. The shock of it all is too much to take as piercing eyes take hold, moving and swaying, she reaches back with great hesitation and with a quick snap, her anatomy for the first time is gazed upon by yearning eyes. Eroticism compounded together with trepidation takes over as monetary compliments formerly known as gratuity is forwarded with great expectations of further exposure. She continues to build momentum towards a new level of debauchery. As the last article of apparel falls gracefully to the floor, she becomes the quintessential ecdysiast swinging from a vertical pillar in such erotic form. As the tension eases, she becomes the hunter instead of the hunted. She takes captive of her audience like the elusive predator pouncing on its prey, only to consume all cognitive senses for the interim. As for her mind and her emotions and all her inhibitions, will not take precedence on this evening. For only the physical aspect of her beauty will be witnessed as the scholar, and the distinguished transcends into the exotic dancer.

Pain in my Heart

Though somewhat intrusive and incumbent upon my soul,
the very essence of my existence is structured as if put on
consignment. The trust susceptible to impotent adolescents,
vulnerable to its coalescence, I am cut down. Impacted by the
trauma of its implications, I continue to grow like a tree by its
natural order in which the deity has intended. I beg for a resolved
answered by a silent whisper. Grasping on to what I don't
completely understand. Carrying the scars of my youth like the
ponderance of some overture. I've reached the age of the majority
standing silently alone in my debauchery. As the Sun starts to
rise, I take in the warmth of it solace like the awakening from a
bad dream or being released from some sort of incarceration. But
just for a moment I bask in its comfort, arbitrary to a capricious
mood of inadequacy. I am the structure who stands before you.
Whimsical in my behavior, always searching for the positive, my
branches reaching out for some relief from this mental anguish. I
take into my lungs a deep breath of gratitude but not to question
why, but to stand like the Mighty Oak as if by itself without a
forest facing the inevitable to one day fall on its own.
Never again to be severed by the hands of such malice.
I will accept my sentence to carry the torch of indignity.
Please Lord, help me deal with this pain in my heart.

The Journey

To see her and hear her song. I am so taken. Her beauty by definition pleases my aesthetic senses to an apogee of emotion contained in my mind and in my heart where she dwells, for she reflects the qualities of perfection, all that is pure and all that is good. As I look into her eyes, I feel a warm embrace yearning to share her thoughts. As she sways, I can see a somewhat forced smile. It reaches so deep for I've never seen anything so sweet. She takes me on a journey to places I've never been, but I can picture in my mind the hillsides in the early spring covered with larkspurs exuberating a botanical coloration creating many different sensations in my mind for her existence remains untouched like an early morning snow before the rising masses leaving the paths unscored by the marks of adulteration. I only wish I could hold you but never to be had like a beautiful blue sky, reaching but not able to touch. I only wish I could know you, my heart can feel absence of my arms, for I miss you but I haven't met you. As the heavens open up, I can hear her song, for the angels couldn't have sent a more beautiful creature. For who is this beauty that can sing, where did she come from but the Heavenly King. I can only believe less what I can see, faith restored from the Bottom of the Sea. Like a light so bright shining on me, that's where she takes me, in my heart she will always be, on a Musical journey that sets me free.

Dedicated to Maci

Bring it Back

Bring back the days when people were singing silhouettes on the
shades and sitting around small city parades. At a time when old
sailors only had tattoos. Anybody else were considered to be fools.
Bring it back to when Cadillacs and Lincolns were the biggest
cars on the road, and a lavatory was more than just a plain old
commode. When men were considered head of the house, and
women normally wore a skirt and a blouse. And yes, most of the
cartoons had something to do with a mouse. Bring it back to a
time when people would smile, and cooking supper usually took
a while. A time when a certain movie star was still in denial, and
most of our celebrities we're not on trial. Bring it back to a time
when families would pray together before a meal, most everything
I had was made out of steel. When the only control stick kids
held in their hands was made out of wood and could hit a ball
deep into the stands. When spending the day at the beach was
considered much fun. When children were allowed to get out and
run. If only we could bring it back to when people appreciated
the simple things in life, when just having enough would have to
suffice. But for now, I'll just have to dream of a day when things
were nice. If you needed a helping hand, nobody would think
twice. When chivalry and class were something that didn't lack.
Oh, I wish I could bring it back.

Move the Chains

So, it begins with an allegiance. Like the Battle Cry at the start of an imperious battle, individual warriors with integers stenciled on their suits of armor. Who will be the autocrat? Like the release of a cannon shot the offense takes its position to receive. The encroachment through enemy's territory is the inevitable plight only to be met with the resistance like an impermeable wall surrounded by a moat. The momentum is temporarily broken. Time to regroup with pugnacious intent, now to align the combative forces. The formation is on the gridiron. The audience anticipation becomes overwhelming, like roman spectators in a coliseum watching on as truculent Gladiators get ready to annihilate the opposition. The play is complete, territory has been taken. The offense has advanced, move the chains! The audience bellows with disruptive intent. Once again, the mood is set, the particle and its antiparticle leaping into the fray. Who will be triumphant? The master of conquest, the offense is on the move with a force to be reckoned with like the start of a rollercoaster ride at an amusement park. The adrenaline builds as the participants reach the pinnacle only to be dropped suddenly as gravity toils petrified souls toward the ground. In the end zone, with this conclusion comes great jubilation and dejection as the victors reap the spoils and those vanquished hear the echoes of their masters, move the chains.

The Ocean

The beautiful sunset reflecting off the shore, a multiple of
seagulls high above they soar. That salty aroma so prevalent
in the air with so much tranquillity, this is my answered
prayer. The feeling of sand surrounding my feet, when water
splashes over them, they sink in so deep. The sound of the
waves splashing all over me, there is just no other place I would
rather be. Living in a world that asks so much, this is what
gets me through, the sea is my crutch. Basking in the sun, this
euphoric sublime, I just wish I could stay here till the end of
time. Just for a moment close your eyes, then dream of a place
that you can surmise. Like taking walks on the beach late at
night and waking up to a beautiful sunrise. An early morning
jog with your favorite dog, waiting for the sun to burn off the
early morning fog. People's greeting as you pass by, a feeling
of contentment that makes me high. At the risk of being
redundant I'll say it again; the ocean is a whole other world that
I need to attend, forever in your heart it will always be penned
like a missed member of your family and your very best friend.

I'm Just Saying

The dictionary's definition of the word belief simply states that it is an acceptance that a statement is true or that something exists. Then how would we have characterized instincts? Well it's defined as an innate fixed pattern of behavior. So, then we would have to conclude anything innate is inborn. That leaves us to believe we don't have control over our instincts the same way we do with something that we choose to believe or not believe. Where am I going with this? As if this wasn't common knowledge. I'm just saying, some are judged by the color of their skin or by their sexual orientation and even their religion. So, what differentiates between the two mentioned is our ability to discern right from wrong and what comes naturally, for it does not come naturally to hate nor it is instinctive. Rather, it is what people choose to believe and then form an opinion. So, then we develop an intolerance for those that hold a different opinion or a viewpoint that differs from oneself, for innate behavior is a fixed action pattern without variation. So, then why do we variate away from what's right or what's going to benefit us, for either way we pay or get paid, for what is good will be a blessing and what is bad will be a malediction. Simple math. I'm just saying, in other words, our abandonment for common sense at times tends to take precedence over what could be beneficial. We then ignore the facts of a given situation which turns into the old adage "we reap what we sow" or "what comes around goes around." So, if we choose to believe that we can judge a person with our eyes without first examining their character, then we have made a choice. For we are not born with instincts that tell us to hate rather its cultural information we received from childhood and throughout adulthood. I'm just saying, from a rhetorical perspective, I asked the question "am I being too analytical?" Well, maybe if we choose to analyze ourselves, we will come to a foregone conclusion that we are not greater than ourselves. Meaning, we are not infallible, no individual is. So, who are we to judge? I'm just saying, if we follow our basic instincts to do what is right and not abandon the greater good that's built in us, there would be no need for war, racial violence, and it would be the end of bigotry. Can you imagine? I'm just saying.

The Ostentatious Demeanor

We are brought up in a certain reciprocity system in which we are taught to control our behavior when it comes to selflessness, or not calling attention to ourselves. For who is it that wants to be defined as pretentious? Even in an exchange of mutual good, we sometimes fine others doing the opposite that leads to a certain level of arrogance. I give you the ostentatious demeanor. As we know, patterns of behavior develop through certain events in one's life, and if you look within ourselves, we find that this is evident. For example, if we get into a regiment of doing what is right for ourselves, we feel rewarded versus the opposite for which there is no reward. For it is easier to stop what is good then what is bad. So, then we need to work on self-improvement or at least monitor our own behavioral patterns. Of course, certain arrogance becomes a filter in that regard. For example, do people find you pleasant and refreshing to be around with? Some develop habits that push people away, and that they're not even aware of or just don't care. And this behavior becomes habitual, sometimes from early childhood on up and could stem from parental behavioral patterns. And even without setting boundaries or having to face consequences, one can safely say that we can develop certain disruptive personality habits that come from worldly interventions and is liking to low self-esteem and even sometimes certain mood disorders. Maybe there's certain unresolved anger issues that's behind it all. But nevertheless, let's fix it. We need to learn that not everything can always go our way. We are not sanctimonious, and there is no need to feel more important or more intelligent than others, for this is usually a cover for insecurity. We need to apply humility and recognize that other people's opinions and thoughts may sometimes differ from our own and we should never impugn their relevance. Neither should we form an opinion of them because of their beliefs. As soon as we can right what is wrong within ourselves, we will grow to a higher level of maturity. Thus, it will make us a more desirable person to be around. Like the changing tides, we need to examine ourselves more closely for there's always room for self-improvement. Life's too short to be caught up in all the bad when there's so much good that can come out of us all.

In the Dawn of such Anguish

Though cognizant of this pain, who would have ever thought of a day that would turn into this adolescent curiosity at such expense? For who is it that expects something so unexpected? So, let's take a walk in these shoes, for one should never feel trapped within oneself for the power of understanding is released by this dissertation. The mental desolation did not precede the physical scars of which one is envisioned by and is likened to shadows of a deeper trauma. For not everything is seen by the power of sight, but by the power of wisdom we can discern a deeper understanding or maybe we can help give back what was taken at the dawn of a life.

A child enjoying his youth is as typical as a bike ride over to a friend's house, but what becomes tragic oscillates between the chaotic and the disbelief of something of this nature. For what unfolds becomes the unimaginable to any parentage so begins the fight for survival as grief turns into the innate healing process. For grief does not destroy one's self-worth, but sadness and anger become the predominant feelings. So begins the fight from the burns caused by the adolescent ignorance of a childhood acquaintance as time tends to heal through reintegration.

There are many different facets of adulthood. For the loss of pride leaves only the silhouettes of one's former self. But the will to rebuild ourselves will reach the level of a stronger proportion, for it is said that only the strongest survive and in the end, that usually is the outcome. For true happiness lives beneath the skin. As is for the individual whose life became the victim also became the triumphant. Through segments of vanishment, a stronger person emerges. And from within me, the writer, for knowing this individual I have grown which gives me a vivid understanding for the person, and the victim in the dawn of such anguish.

The Miracle of Me

As I awake in the morning, I slowly come to the realization of my life. The all to incurable, the miracle of me. My senses are somewhat reputed. My body starts to become one with the pleasures of my rapture. Erotic as it may be, my soul captivates me. I am alive! I can feel my toes attached to my feet, and my hands. My God! The touch is so sweet!

I become enthralled with this enchanting treat, my emotional turmoil at its highest peak. I'm at the critical point of this apogee. I celebrate the spectacle, the miracle of me. The temporary sensation of anything I have to do, I asked the question can this be true? I am the physical being of my epitome, I am just so overtaken by the miracle of me. Now, hold your applause but it's safe to say, I'm so consumed by its Arabic bouquet. The all to impervious, what a sweet display, without it, my life would be in complete disarray. I bask in the stimulus that has overtaken me, that feeling of euphoria, the impetus, that is key. Oh, my good Lord I'm so thankful to be, I celebrate your blessing, the miracle of me. Now as the Sun starts to rise as if someone's blatant surprise, my feeling of contentment no longest survives. Now I must leave this sanctuary although it's been kind, yes, it's time to put my nose to the grind. In order to repeat this peaceful sublime, I'll have to make it to work, hopefully on time. Now it's about the hour to pay that comparable fee, and continue to celebrate the miracle of me.

The Bar

Yes, the famous cliché, a place to go where everybody knows your name. The working class making their claim to fame. The public entourage without significance, having one too many is my predicament. A Home of social indifference inspired by the toxic elixir, If I buy her one more, maybe I can kiss her. Oh, my God, I think she's going to lift up her bra, don't worry honey! With me, you'll go far. My biggest concern I would hate for this shining star? My intoxicated visual getting kicked out of the bar. Described as an adult beverage or some sort of shot, so it is said enough of this stuff, and your stomach will rot.

The evening cocktail not to impugn the definition of the word, which is some sort of fruit appetizer the comparison is absurd. Oh, yes! The implications of such repetition, that leads us all to that euphoric condition. The most recognized popularity contest hosted by me, the end result is no nominee. A pageant with spectators' absence of the crowning Jewel, and bottoms up is the only golden rule. Where fluid spirits can rise us up bigger than we are, you know where I'm headed, it's off to the bar. Bartender please pour me a shot of that confection, that eases my mind for a more positive connection. Where friends can be made and tabs aren't always paid, a sanctuary for most, here's to you I make a toast.

I raise my glass to the things I celebrate this day, like everyone else there goes my hard-earned pay. People will come and people will go, some stay a while, they become family you know. Like some big reunion at the end of the year, I look forward to seeing you and drinking a beer. Last call has been announced where did it all go, I enjoyed your company, you put on one hell of a show. I hope in your travels you won't be far, the next time you're in town, we'll meet at the bar.

In My Thoughts Every Day

From the time of conception God's gift to us both, the sanctity between a man and a woman, bound by its scriptural oath. I gaze upon this marvel, whom I love more with each day, if I seem to care too much, as to push you away. Love is not selfish, nor impudent in any way, mine will always be with you, in my thoughts every day. Like walking on a beach so refreshing is the sea, a beautiful sunset, looking over at me. Like a moment in passing, I just want it to stay, you're in my thoughts every day. The trees in the summer, bountiful with so many leaves, the greenery so vivid, they sway in the breeze. I can feel a comforting spirit, I asked of this day, I pray to you God, incessantly this way. Oh, my dear Lord hear my ardent plea, watch over and protect her, she's so precious to me. Time has passed, the baby has grown, from a child to a woman, how fast it has flown. Just remember, no matter where you go or how far away we part, know deep down in your beautiful heart, you'll always be with me in my thoughts until I die, and sometimes my words may make you cry. I need you to know that I love you more than words could ever say, you will be in my thoughts every day.

Another Day in The Life

Sometimes awkward in my intentions, beguiled by the dogma
that is set by each Sunrise. I set forth to conquer the world
that is before me. The existence of the corporate metaphor
that continues to thrive on behalf of its constituents. I
unwillingly engage in the transit of its nature to accomplish
the Intrepid of my endeavor, as if, one vernacular represented
a constitutional purpose that is imposed but not enforced. I
must survive! The struggle between the classes, the onslaught
of monetary gain without a conscience, and the diabolical
phenomenon that continue to infiltrate my existence
controlled by the substance of its own Peril. I must continue!
The hour is upon me asking for a result. Everything is black
and white without merit. I am consumed and ostracized
by the most fortunate. Labeled as if the produce is placed
conveniently in its containment. I continue to thrive as the day
becomes weak. The onslaught of fortitude compounded by the
love of my fleshly existence. I continue on as if someone was
beckoning me to reach for the finish line. Black-and-white
seemingly becomes color as if fireworks were ignited into the
air with a ponderance of beauty and elegance. I have reached
the apogee of this day, with the culmination of my success, I
am triumphant! I have survived yet another day in the life.

If I Should Stumble

From the day I saw you I knew you were special, a spirit so lively captured in such a beautiful vessel. Good enough for you I thought I could never be, you proved me wrong, by being with me. Now time has passed and many years have gone by, and yes there are times when I made you cry. But God put us together for reasons that we don't always understand, love is more complicated than a ring on your hand. If it seems that I have become somewhat complacent, nobody ever, could be your replacement. It's just that, there are days when I'm tired and down, and not much of an expression, just this weary old frown. If you feel that the romance or my attraction for you is gone, let me explain this, you couldn't be more wrong. Now the human heart beats close to a hundred times a minute, deep within mine you'll always be in it. And over a lifetime somewhere around three billion, and as long as I'm with you, I hope it's a trillion. Forever my bond with you, will be tightly knit, like the vows we shared, I could never remit. And as long as I'm living, and being with you, the words I say, will always be true. For the beautiful person that my life I have shared, there's never a day, that I haven't cared. For God bless us both that our home always be humble, and please my love forgive me, if I should stumble.

The Color of Money

Since I was a young boy I was taught to value, and live a good life and not be shallow. The infallible heroes they will always be, composed on paper for all to see. It seems these days nobody can get enough, it's just so hard to accumulate the stuff. Now don't get me wrong soon after I was born, the clothes I had were faded and torn. My grandmother would sew patches on the elbows and knees, the sultans of survival on soup and grilled cheese. Now that I'm older and able to earn, I take from childhood the lessons I had learned. The tangible items, the things that thieves steal, think about it people, it's time to get real. Anything accumulated from material wealth, could never take the place of having good health. Now let me give you the invaluable spiel, not the things collected that the eyes can appeal. It's the love of family and friends, the values that are rife, there is nothing you can take, at the end of your life. Now the wisdom that you discern from my words in turn, will bring about happiness in the years to yearn. And all your days may they be sunny, if we can all get past the color of money.

A Girl and a Woman

So, what begins with a story, the verbal epigram stimulated by the vista of this tangible site. I implore you to recognize my observance. Her eyes tell a story far beyond the mystique and beauty emphasized by her character. Tortuous with an enlightening twist. Flamboyant with an overwhelming cachet of exuberance and personality. Followed by her somewhat coltish behavior, I am amused and entertained creating the impetus of a largely dynamic proportion. Never indecorous are my thoughts. I cannot help but wonder what is it, the kittenish smile, her vivacious ora, I give you the girl, named after a favorable season, partly because of its rewarding comfort after a long assiduous transitive. So fitting is the frolic followed by the warmth of her embrace, I give you the woman, a tad bit complex when in vogue, her visual expression is somewhat Prada, quintessence by definition. The grand spectacle of this apotheosis allures and is deserving of any man's attention. To summarize the characteristics of her compelling mortality would be insatiable. For in her eyes I see the perfect amalgam when she becomes transit between... a girl and a woman

Is There a Place that They All Go?

I cannot remember saying goodbye and really ever meaning it. Why can I not see them such a loss you would permit. See the moments are few and the time is short all the days that we have spent. Aren't we all the Angels that together you had sent? Why so many, from me, you have chosen to take back. My heart toils with so much loss, the absence of those that were part of me at such an emotional cost. My heart feels so defiled as if someone broke into my sole and stole what was mine. Please help me understand as to how I've missed your sign. So, then I asked you for the wisdom to help me to discern. There is so much to wonder about it's really a big concern. Is there a place that they all go, does your heavenly light shine on them like a warm summer day? Can they still see your wonderful creations in any sort of way? Like a beautiful waterfall in a sub-tropical place or an island by the sea. Can you tell them to look down on me? Please hear my incessant plea. Is there an abundance of Peace has the pain released? Please give me some sort of clue, as my tears fall down, I need to know if this can possibly be true. But for now, I'll pray and, in a way, I feel your comforting spirit. Please help me Lord to stand up strong because I can hardly bear it. I know it may take time to understand and realize that there is a better place, so one day when he calls for me, I'll see your beautiful face. And thank you Lord for helping me for deep down I think we all know, with your heavenly grace when we shall pass, I know where we will all go.

Just One More Day

I miss them so much,
my parents and my brother.
I just need to say,
I wish I could be with you,
just one more day.
All the memories of our childhood
and the times we were together
stored deeply in my heart always and forever.
Early spring, we would take walks
and sometimes we would run and hide,
such a beautiful family,
with so much pride.
My parents bought used bikes,
they taught us to ride,
I felt so safe with them by my side.
We would play softball, my father would pitch,
we didn't have much but together we were rich.
My fondest memories of us at the beach,
and all the lessons only a mother could teach.
If I could go back,
this is what I would say,
I love and miss you all so much,
and I would give anything,
for just one more day.

The New Bar Rules

Leave hate at the door, and be prepared for the invincible tour. Now, sometimes people think that life has no purpose, that time spent on this earth is nothing but worthless. But let me ask you, my friend, to sit down and converse, even if the vernacular is somewhat diverse. The stress of the world can weigh on us hard, sadness and tragedy that leaves us tired and marred. So, let me lay on you the new bar rules, happiness and contentment sit only on these stools. Where our hearts are open, this ain't no bull, the joys of life are shared in full. Regardless of race, religion, or creed, avarice people, the definition of greed. We're all here to share in the real riches of this world, the true human experience and anything less, out the door its hurled. For the short time we're here, I'd rather celebrate with you, smiles and laughter, genuine and true. And to bring out nothing but the good deep down in so many, a quandary of cheer tossed around like confetti. Now these are the new bar rules honest and true, come on in, I raise my glass to you.

The Sight of Color

Like that of a rainbow during a sultry day in a transitional rainforest. I visualize a sublime fantasy of an uncanny retrospective in all my vigor, walking through the woods of Grace, observing a natural wonder in which not all of creation can discern. I picture a volcano in an explosive stage spewing out a wide range of an illuminist liquid turning into the solid of which nature can induce all of its natural beauty. The vivid blue sky on a clear summer's day when all is in bloom, I see the green, the Reds, the yellows all simultaneously creating an abstract conceptual. For a moment put asunder all the pain in your heart discontented by the black and white of a world controlled by the frivolous. We become colorblind by the arbitrary imposition taking away from the autumn exuberance in which our soul can bask. Now dive into the ocean of Tranquility sinking down as deep as the coral reef and become enthralled by the wonderous colors of its natural habitat in which piece of mind can thrive. The well-being of the human experience, and in the garden of the origin of life in which hope will one day be restored. The gift of sight, can you imagine one day without it! Through a visual cortex we become the affluent, not in the monetary but by the things taken for granted that could never be replaced by what is the perception of wealth. For in this world the tangible iridescent brought on by the spectrum of enlightenment gives way to a new beginning and forever filled with cheer and vitality brought on only by the sight of color.

Mellifluous Speech

Euphoria is the sound of her voice but true altruism and
Fidelity is the component that makes up the substance of
which she is. Like a sound of a soft rain in the early morning
that stimulates your senses, exalted with an overwhelming
sense of comfort flowing through your body like a rushing
river in the early part of the spring coming down from a
Mountaintop after an agonist winter. Passion by her veracity
she speaks to me in a rhythm that's far from prosaic, yet
metrical with such ferocity that without her presence I feel the
improvisation deep within my soul. I visualize this beautiful
form that presents itself with such tenacity that I become
gallant as I bask in her beauty. I am forced to compose the
visual into an audio fixation that from within me I can hear
the smooth flowing sound that spins me into a euphoric
sublime brought on by her mellifluous speech

The Unseen Heroes

The dictionary defines a Hero as a person with distinguished courage and ability at their own personal risk and danger. A Hero can come in many forms and when we're young we look up to certain athletic achievers we call heroes, but some have certain indiscretions that make us question ourselves as to who really is worthy of being called a Hero. There's one who makes the ultimate sacrifice by laying down one's life to save others. I give you the Unseen Hero, for the very freedoms that we all have come at a cost beyond the monetary definition we call compensation. So why is it that we deserve this protection without ever knowing the persons representing us in such a menacing society? Here's an example, in order to achieve world peace, everyone in the world population would have to behave in the manner which all people would respect the rights and freedom of others, but, in the real world we know that the majority of the population can't be trusted with that sort of responsibility. Hence, in order to avoid total world devastation, we rely on the Unseen Heroes to protect us and to bring the world into order. We don't always know them by name nor by face but they are out there fighting the most invidious people who try to take away our very freedoms, whether it be on the streets, in our cities and towns or fighting overseas to protect our country. So why am I carrying on about all of this? Sometimes, we just need a reminder of the things that don't consume us as much as living in this contemporary society we call home. For all that we have, and everything tangible that we need for the fulfillment of our happiness came at a price which not all of us are willing to pay but by tremendous sacrifices of the men and women who serve, the Unseen Heroes.

Restless

The darkness of night covers over me like the cinders of some combustible force. Cogent and enthralling my eyes stare into the confinement of it subjugates. I glance at the digital Integer in its relentless pursuit to reach the final summation of the inevitable kindle. I must sleep in a silent cry boasted from my conscience begging for solace. The marathon continues as if inadvertently auspicious to a higher diabolical power deliberating my insurrection against this army. I instruct my militia to forward into battle against the restraint that overwhelmingly influences my dilemma. The tedious repetition of my physical repositioning, the mines obstreperous conflict continues to alter my circadian instincts as I await my vindication from this ongoing interlude. Finally, a subliminal auditory penetrates the front line breaking into the fray, causing the noose to give way. I am released from the bondage of this incarceration. As my body starts to lose consciousness, I am interrupted by a daunting audio. The sole purpose of this vendetta is now obstructed, defeated, as I am compromised by the awakening stratagem, solely purposed to defy the natural order of one's ebullience. Too late for an appeal, the jury has reached its verdict. Sentence has been rendered on to me as I accept my fate. For this morning I am restless.

A Potential Man I could Be

When I was born and as the angels looked on, my blessings were these, because my mother was strong. And through her beautiful eyes, I knew that she could see the potential man I could be. When I was a boy, I felt so secure because being a courageous loving woman was a virtue to her. Through my eyes I could see by the examples of her, the potential man that I could be. And as I grew from a boy to a man, there were days I felt I could no longer stand, there she was to give me a hand, because she believed in me, the potential man I could be. Now that she is gone, and almost like the words of a song, I hear a whispering voice telling me to be strong. Because of her love and kindness, I overcame my blindness. Because she believed in me, I became a potential man I could be.

A Truck Driver

What begins from childhood the imaginary dream, with toys
that resemble something so extreme, that one day when I'm
older, my boyish fantasy will redeem, driving down the road in
a monstrosity of a machine. All alone in my solitude it seems I
haven't talked for days, the people that I love, I miss in so many
ways. Forever it seems I've been on this road, when the weather
gets rough, may I be so bold. My job is to deliver, I'm the
quintessential giver, of all the things we need, done respectively
with speed. Now I'm stuck in traffic, how could this be, a
hundred miles of cars and trucks as far as the eye can see. Lord,
grant me the patience to deal with this mess, not moving along
brings on so much stress. The places I have gone, the things
that I have seen, I have no regrets, I'm living the dream. Now
some view us as an overall cussing regime, and long hair and
beards is the familiar scene. We are town to town like royalty
wearing a crown, hoping and praying we don't break down.
Supplying all the necessities is what we do, we give it our all,
honest and true. We are long-distance survivors and down like a
deep-sea diver, don't forget to thank, a truck driver.

Time to Wake

Quite is the morning, until the sound of the audacious fowl announcing their existence upon the dawn of creation through an audio fixation that stimulates my senses. I become overwhelmed by the sudden affliction with a ponderance of thought, almost intrusive as I become aware of my mortality in such an awkward manner. I start to discriminate my conscience. How it makes cowards of us all! I must arbitrarily coexist against my better judgment to remain docile to this comforting tranquility. Please, just for a few minutes more as I stare directly into the motionless inorganic matter. No longer is there a verbal audio as my mind begins to concede to the inevitable, refusing to give in to the fears conjured up in my very own mind. The insecurities of being as if I were a small animal that could fall prey to an elusive predator. So many thoughts all at once overtaken by the moral seeds of my soul to plant me in the soil of truth, only to sprout out with anxiety is if leaves opening up for the first time in its rightful season. All right I get it, like something screaming at me, as if my very existence depends on this moment. I must deal with this somatic material that it's me, to rise and put asunder my body in this place of rest for I must concede to this annoying ringtone. Like a gun going off at the start of a race, in an instant I become mobile and leap Into the fray that is the start of my day. Naked and vulnerable, my hands reach for the stimulus that propels my flesh into the mechanical substance of which I am, and in this daunting hour, humbling the deafening of this silence. It is time to wake.

A Best Friend

By definition, a friend is best described as one having a bond of mutual affection. A best friend is described as someone most close to you. I give you my synopsis in four components. The human element, always the first when you make plans, someone you can always trust, who shares mutual interest. Someone that will gain knowledge and educate oneself for the sole purpose of being able to share in the other one's interests. The perception element, the ability to look inside the other person, cognizant of their pain, their happiness, the ability to discern their thoughts through the mirrors of one's eyes that cleverly disguises a quandary of self-inflicted inadequacies, keeping in mind that mirrors reflect only what you see, overlooking any criticisms that might alter one's normal comportment. The humility element, the ability to recognize one strength without resentful longing. The fortitude to recognize capabilities void of any gratuitous emotions yet bask proudly in the others accomplishments. The compatible element. The ability to harmonize in such a way that enjoyment is able to exuberate without the wasteful intolerance of conflict. Being able to maintain a relationship filled with ebullience and time well spent, recognizing the quality of life shared by true definition of a best friend.

The Weight of the World

As I get older, I'm bothered by the fact that there is never enough time. No matter what you need to accomplish, time waits for no one and neither does your boss making time your unspoken enemy. I mean, think about it, from the time you get up in the morning till the time you go to bed you're constantly trying to beat the clock. You feel like you're carrying around the weight of the world trying to get through yet another day. Life just seems to be an intrusion, taking you out of your comfort zone. So then, what happens? STRESS! Do you ever notice that when it comes to the weekend, though time seems to pass quicker, you're more relaxed and you can get into a routine that suits your comfort level considering you're not overwhelmed with household chores. But wait! Come Monday, your total routine changes which causes room for error! Have you ever noticed if you have a pet, especially a dog, that animal needs to follow a routine. If you take the dog out of the routine then accidents seem to happen. Are we any different? On top of all that, we have to deal with financial situations that leave us uneasy, illnesses, death and so many other things that come our way compounded by taking care of the needs of others. Most of us are able to cope with it, as long as we can take a sabbatical every now and again allowing us to take a load off so to speak. Yes, to lift the weight of the world off our shoulders, we need to ESCAPE! Well, how do we do that? Let me give you some examples. For one, you have to have a hobby, which is one way to get out of your own head. Some people enjoy meditation and others turn to the gym as physical fitness is one of the bigger and better stress relievers when it comes to carrying around the weight of everyday life. I myself have been into physical fitness most of my life and find it better than taking medication for things such as depression and fatigue. However, sometimes we can't find the time for that so how about this! Try reading a couple pages a day from a book that might capture your interest. I find that reading, writing poetry and short stories puts me back in a comfort zone that helps relieve stress. I can see you've already gotten started on the reading thing because you're reading my book. I would like to congratulate you on making a great choice towards a better quality of life! I hope you enjoy reading my poetry and short stories as much as I enjoy writing them. So then let's continue on, shall we?

A Poem
to a Very Special Friend

Can you believe another year has passed by;
I hope your happiness on this day is as vast as the stars in the sky.
How special it was on that day you see,
a beautiful baby girl, that came to be.
And then, she blossomed and grew,
to become the person, The Wonderful You.
I just wanted to say to a young lady I admire so much
for all the hearts you've touched and always helping those as such.
Happy 13th birthday Jadyn my friend,
my love and respect will never end.

"It doesn't matter how many times you fail in life
as long as you believe in yourself"

John Bouley